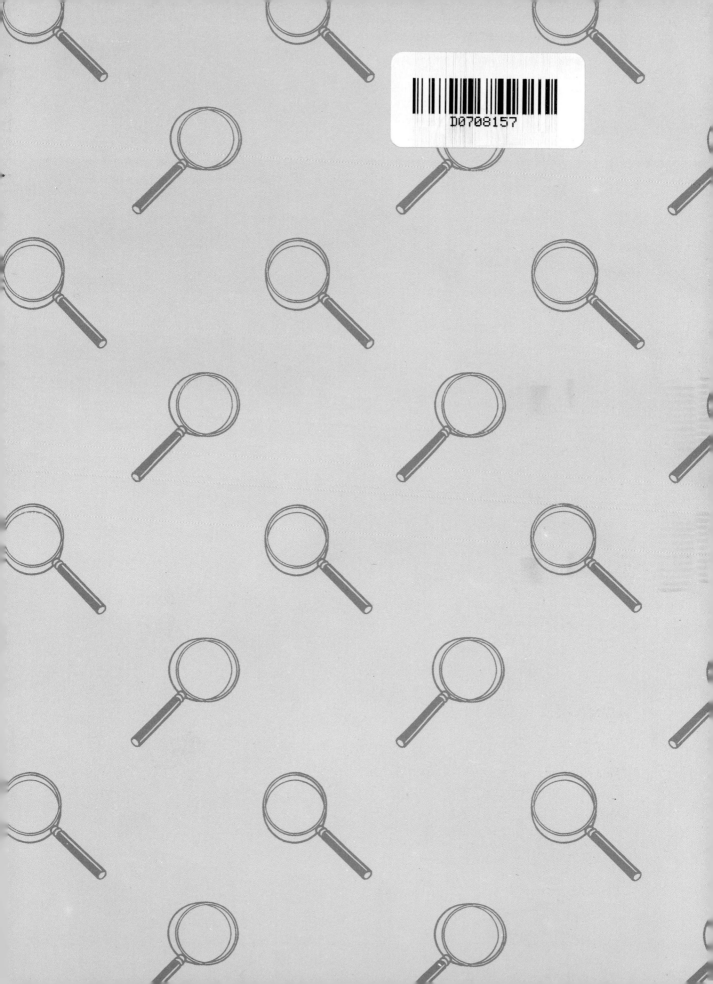

ISBN 0-86163-485-3

Copyright © 1986 by Templar Publishing Ltd.

First published in Great Britain by
Macdonald & Co (Publishers) Ltd.

This edition first published 1991 by
Award Publications Limited,
Spring House, Spring Place,
Kentish Town, London NW5 3BH

Printed in Singapore

MIGHTY MAMMALS OF THE PAST

Written by
JOHN STIDWORTHY
MA Cantab

Consultant Editor
STEVE PARKER
BSc Zoology

Illustrated by
CHRIS FORSEY

AWARD PUBLICATIONS

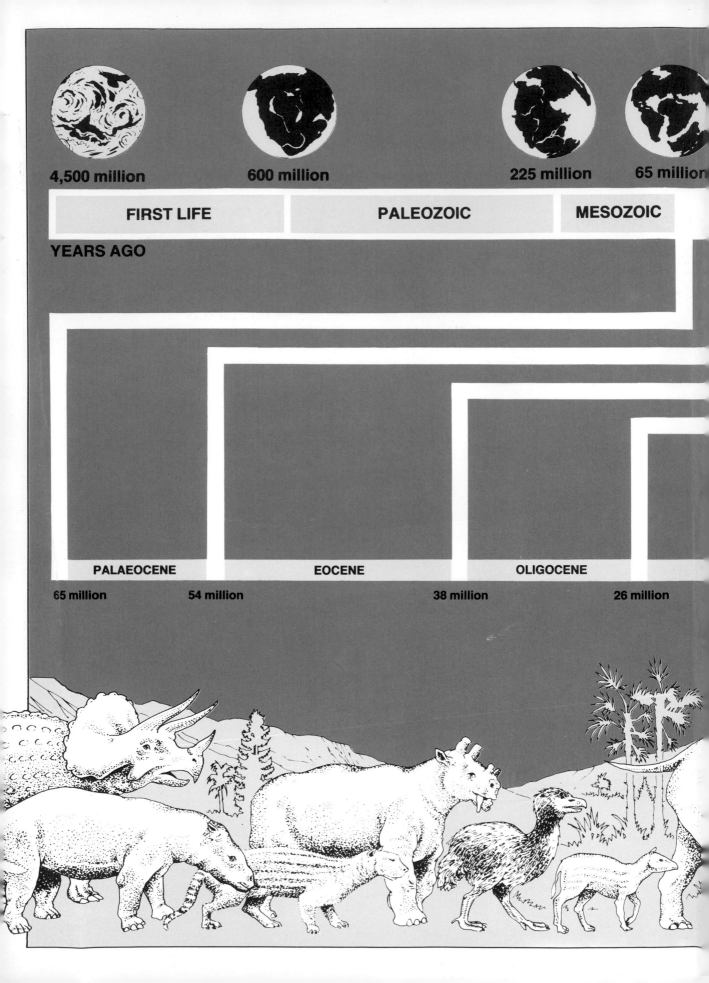

4,500 million

600 million

225 million

65 million

FIRST LIFE

PALEOZOIC

MESOZOIC

YEARS AGO

PALAEOCENE

EOCENE

OLIGOCENE

65 million

54 million

38 million

26 million

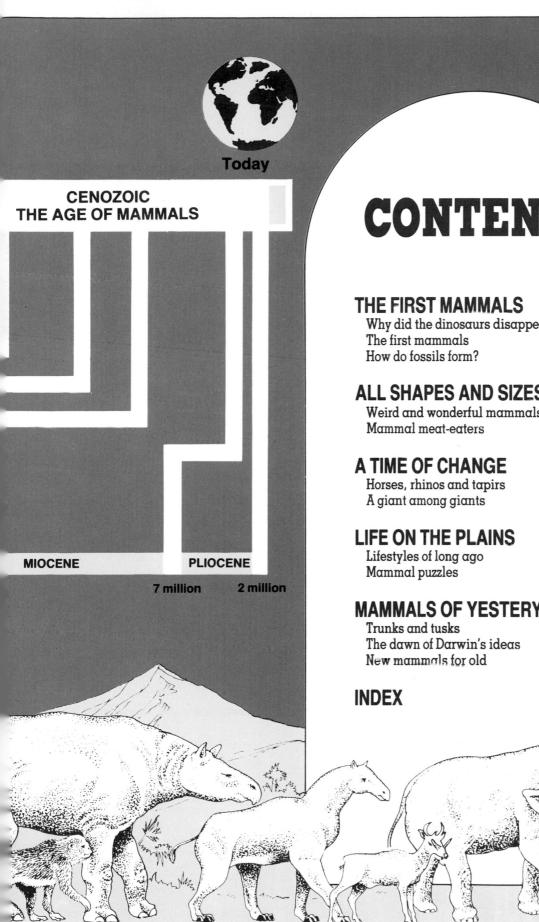

Today

**CENOZOIC
THE AGE OF MAMMALS**

MIOCENE   PLIOCENE

7 million   2 million

CONTENTS

THE FIRST MAMMALS

Sixty-five million years ago, dinosaurs suddenly became extinct. How suddenly we may never know. It was quick in terms of the fossil record in the rocks, but it happened so long ago that it's almost impossible for us to tell if they died out over a few months or thousands of years.

What is certain is that the dinosaurs, which had been the biggest, most successful and probably the brainiest animals to live on this planet for more than 100 million years, were completely wiped out. Many other living things also died, including over half the plants and lots of the surface-dwelling sea creatures. But some things managed to survive, and the disappearance of the dinosaurs provided them with a great opportunity to take over the Earth. The creatures that took this opportunity were the mammals.

Mammals were already around during and even before the Age of Dinosaurs. But they were mostly small, nocturnal animals that spent their time scampering through the undergrowth or climbing trees in order to hide from the hunting dinosaurs. Mammals seemed to have no way of challenging the dinosaurs for supremacy. But once the dinosaurs disappeared, they got their chance. Mammals quickly took over the land and became the dominant animals. The last 65 million years – and perhaps the next few million – are all part of the Age of Mammals.

The first mammals

We may not know why the dinosaurs died out. But do we know why mammals took over? Before we can answer that question, we must decide what a mammal is. The main features to look out for are shown on the right. Most important is the fact that mammals are warm-blooded. They keep their bodies at a constant temperature, and are ready for action at all times, and in all weather. The reptiles (including the dinosaurs) were cold-blooded and needed to soak up heat energy from the sun before they could move about. Lots of them were very big so they absorbed heat slowly, but once they became warm they had no way of cooling themselves down if the climate became too hot. This could be why the mammals survived 65 million years ago while the dinosaurs perished through overheating or by being frozen to death.

Although fossils can't tell us if a pre-historic animal was warm-blooded, they do give us a few clues. By looking at an animal's bones – the main parts usually preserved as fossils – we can often work out whether or not it was a mammal.

You can see from the chart below that scientists have found a whole series of fossil animals which gradually change from reptiles to mammals. We must draw a line somewhere and say: 'All animals with these features are mammals.' Most fossil experts agree that if an animal is found to have a single bone for its lower jaw and three small bones in each ear, then we can call it a mammal.

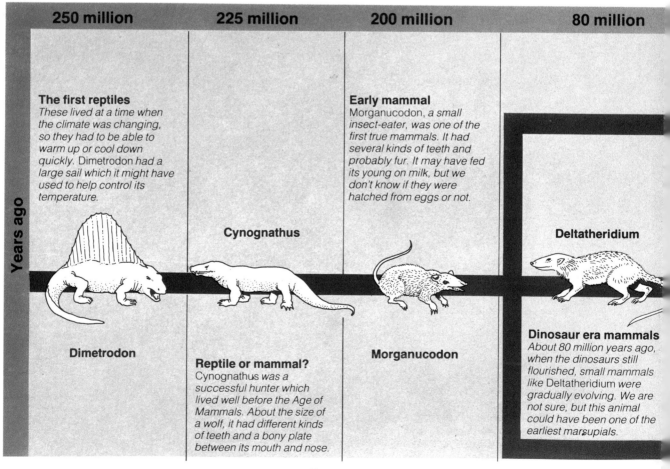

| 250 million | 225 million | 200 million | 80 million |

Years ago

The first reptiles
These lived at a time when the climate was changing, so they had to be able to warm up or cool down quickly. Dimetrodon had a large sail which it might have used to help control its temperature.

Cynognathus

Early mammal
Morganucodon, *a small insect-eater, was one of the first true mammals. It had several kinds of teeth and probably fur. It may have fed its young on milk, but we don't know if they were hatched from eggs or not.*

Deltatheridium

Dimetrodon

Reptile or mammal?
Cynognathus *was a successful hunter which lived well before the Age of Mammals. About the size of a wolf, it had different kinds of teeth and a bony plate between its mouth and nose.*

Morganucodon

Dinosaur era mammals
About 80 million years ago, when the dinosaurs still flourished, small mammals like Deltatheridium *were gradually evolving. We are not sure, but this animal could have been one of the earliest marsupials.*

What is a mammal?

Here is a typical mammal. It has fur, keeps warm and stays active, but to do this it needs lots of fuel (food) and a continuous supply of oxygen (from the air). The bony plate which separates the nose from the mouth means it can breathe and chew at the same time, for oxygen and food. Also it gives birth to babies, instead of laying eggs like a reptile. The babies are cared for and fed with milk by the mother. These and many other improvements over the reptiles meant that mammals could take over the world 65 million years ago.

Single bone for lower jaw

Three small bones in ear to amplify sounds and improve hearing

Bony plate between nose and mouth allows animal to breathe and eat at the same time

Different teeth are shaped for different jobs, so almost any food can be eaten

Large brain and intelligent behaviour

Fur keeps body heat in

In a placental mammal, the young are born quite well-formed and are fed on milk from the mother's nipples

Legs are below body, making support and movement easier

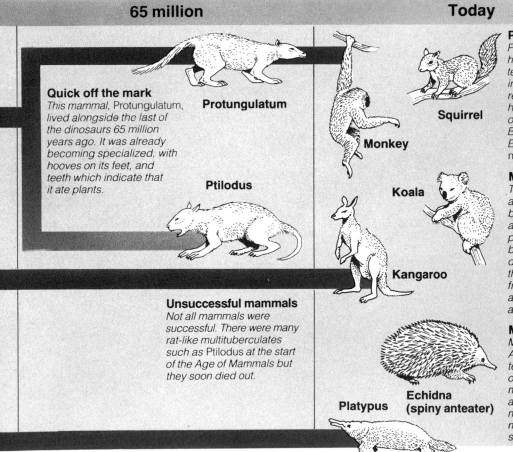

65 million   **Today**

Protungulatum

Quick off the mark
This mammal, Protungulatum, lived alongside the last of the dinosaurs 65 million years ago. It was already becoming specialized, with hooves on its feet, and teeth which indicate that it ate plants.

Ptilodus

Unsuccessful mammals
Not all mammals were successful. There were many rat-like multituberculates such as Ptilodus at the start of the Age of Mammals but they soon died out.

Monkey

Squirrel

Koala

Kangaroo

Platypus

Echidna (spiny anteater)

Placental mammals
Placental mammals have a high, constant body temperature. Babies develop in the mother's womb and receive nourishment from her blood through a special organ called the placenta. Babies are born well formed. Examples are cats, dogs, monkeys and humans.

Marsupial mammals
These live only in Australia and South America. Their body temperature is lower and varies more than that of placentals. The young are born very early in their development and crawl to the mother's pouch to feed from her nipple. Examples are kangaroos, opossums and koala bears.

Monotreme mammals
Monotremes only live in Australia. Their body temperature is between that of placentals and marsupials. They lay eggs and have a different type of milk gland from other mammals. They have many similarities to reptiles.

Who was Cuvier?
Frenchman Georges Cuvier (1769 – 1832) was the first real palaeontologist (fossil expert). He had an amazing knowledge of living creatures, on which he based his fossil work. He was able to tell which fossil mammals were related to living ones, and deduce appearances from a single bone.

How do fossils form?

Most dead animals and plants are eaten or rot away, leaving no trace of their existence. Just occasionally, however, an animal dies and its body somehow ends up in a river or swamp, where it is soon covered by mud and buried. Even then the body may decay but, if conditions are right, the hard parts like bones and teeth will be preserved. For thousands or millions of years they stay there – until one day they are discovered by a lucky fossil-hunter. Fossils, then, are the remains of long-dead animals and plants.

Hard parts such as bones and teeth may be unchanged when they are dug up, thousands of years after the animal has died. But usually chemical changes will have taken place, even though the size and shape of the original will have been preserved. Minerals seep in and harden the bone tissues, or water dissolves away the original material, replacing it with new minerals. Sometimes the bone is completely dissolved away, leaving only a hole in the rock. Later, this hole may be filled by a different material seeping into it, filling the place of the original remains. Rarely, a whole animal is preserved, trapped in amber or pickled in natural tar.

As well as the remains of actual animals, scientists have also discovered another type of fossil, called a trace fossil. This is a preserved trace or sign of an animal rather than the creature itself. Footprints, the marks where it rested or fed, or even fossil droppings are all trace fossils.

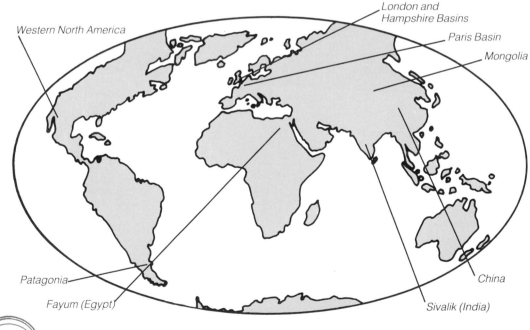

Western North America

London and Hampshire Basins

Paris Basin

Mongolia

Patagonia

China

Fayum (Egypt)

Sivalik (India)

Where to look for fossils

Fossils are usually found in sedimentary rocks formed from the mud in lakes, rivers and seas. Look for fossil-bearing rocks in cliffs, riverbanks and road cuttings, but do be careful as these places can be dangerous. Remember, too, that you may need permission to visit quarries and cuttings.

The fossils described in this book nearly all come from fairly 'new' rocks – formed in the last 65 million years. If you go looking for fossils, you are more likely to find those of sea creatures such as shellfish, since mammal fossils are rare. Those embedded in rocks will have to be removed with a geological hammer. Try and split the rocks along natural breaks, or else you'll probably just destroy them.

The making of fossils

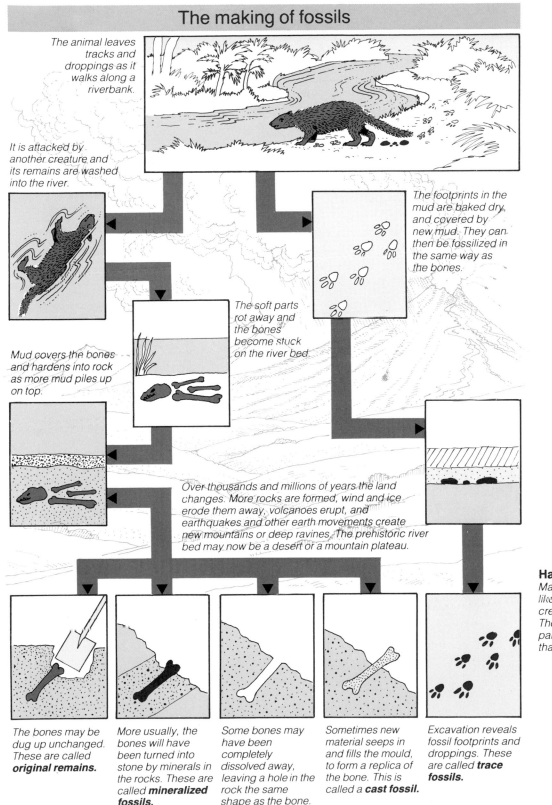

The animal leaves tracks and droppings as it walks along a riverbank.

It is attacked by another creature and its remains are washed into the river.

The footprints in the mud are baked dry, and covered by new mud. They can then be fossilized in the same way as the bones.

The soft parts rot away and the bones become stuck on the river bed.

Mud covers the bones and hardens into rock as more mud piles up on top.

Over thousands and millions of years the land changes. More rocks are formed, wind and ice erode them away, volcanoes erupt, and earthquakes and other earth movements create new mountains or deep ravines. The prehistoric river bed may now be a desert or a mountain plateau.

The bones may be dug up unchanged. These are called **original remains.**

More usually, the bones will have been turned into stone by minerals in the rocks. These are called **mineralized fossils.**

Some bones may have been completely dissolved away, leaving a hole in the rock the same shape as the bone. This is called a **mould fossil.**

Sometimes new material seeps in and fills the mould, to form a replica of the bone. This is called a **cast fossil.**

Excavation reveals fossil footprints and droppings. These are called **trace fossils.**

Hard teeth

Mammal teeth are the likeliest fossils of these creatures to be found. They are the hardest parts and last longer than bones.

ALL SHAPES AND SIZES

Fifty million years ago, during the early Eocene period, the dinosaurs had all disappeared. But their place was quickly filled by mammals of all shapes and sizes. Birds, too, evolved rapidly. Giant flightless birds like *Diatryma* stalked the Earth, probably attacking and eating small mammals. But the birds soon lost the battle for supremacy on the ground, and mammals became the main land animals.

Although many mammals from 50 million years ago were quite different from those alive now, their surroundings were becoming increasingly like our own. The flowers and trees were similar to the varieties alive nowadays, and much of the Earth was forest. There were no wide, grassy plains, though, since grasses had not yet appeared.

Eocene fossils have given us clues which tell us that many parts of the world were much warmer than they are today. Warmth-loving fig trees and magnolias lived in Alaska. Crocodiles and turtles swam among palm trees in the swamps of southern England. And in most of Britain the climate was like Malaysia's is now.

Compared to modern mammals, many Eocene mammals look odd and clumsy. But we must remember that evolution works slowly, and that these animals were fairly new to their way of life. We can think of them as 'experimental' mammals which evolution was trying out in a world suddenly free of dinosaurs.

Mammal meat-eaters

As more and more mammals came along they took to new ways of life. Some groups evolved to become plant-eaters, or *herbivores*, grazing in herds or browsing on the leaves of trees. It wasn't long before other mammals worked out that the herbivores themselves were a new source of food. So the meat-eaters, or *carnivores*, evolved.

Over millions of years the carnivores generally became bigger, so that they could tackle larger prey. They also developed large, sharp teeth so they could catch hold of and cut up their victims. Many carnivores that were a success during most of the Eocene belonged to one particular group – the *creodonts*.

The word creodont means 'flesh tooth'. The creodonts evolved from the small, insect-eating mammals like *Deltatheridium*, which were alive at the time of the last dinosaurs. During the Eocene, creodonts gradually became larger, and their teeth became bigger and sharper for dealing with meat. They developed big slicing, *carnassial*, teeth at the back of their mouths to act as shears for cutting tough skin and flesh.

Most creodonts had long, low heads with room for only a small, primitive brain. So they were probably not very clever. Many also had the old-fashioned type of mammal feet, where the sole and five toes were placed flat on the ground. A few stood up on their toes – a more advanced design for fast running.

As evolution continued the old-fashioned, slow and clumsy herbivores gradually disappeared or changed into quicker, cleverer versions. It is thought that the creodonts, which had a fairly primitive design and small brains, could not keep up with the changes. They gradually died out, and by 38 million years ago were nearly all extinct. Scientific evidence shows that modern meat-eaters actually evolved from a different mammal group called *fissipeds*.

Fight for food

Here a creodont *lives up to its 'flesh tooth' name. A* Tritemnodon *sets about making a meal of a* Notharctus.

Patriofelis

Oxyaenids

The oxyaenids were one of the two main groups of creodonts. They had short, squat skulls, short legs and flat feet which probably ended in blunt, rounded claws. *Oxyaena*, which gave its name to the group, was about the size of a badger but slimmer (see page 12). It could have killed animals up to the size of a rabbit, and possibly tried to catch larger prey. *Patriofelis*, shown here, was a medium-sized, cat-like creodont. *Megistotherium* was a giant creodont as big as a rhino. It was one of the few members of the creodont group to survive until the Miocene, 20 million years ago, and can be seen on page 27.

Hyaenodontids

This group of creodonts had long skulls and jaws and tended to stand on their toes. They were generally fairly small. *Hyaenodon* was one member of the group, and is shown on page 18. *Tritemnodon* (on the right) was another – a very slim, muscular animal which could probably outrun most other creatures of its time.

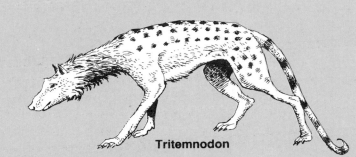

Tritemnodon

What is it?

Mesonyx was another primitive meat-eater. It was once thought to be the ancestor of modern carnivorous mammals, which are in the group called *Carnivora*. Then scientists changed their minds and put this creature into the creodont group. More recently opinions have changed again. Scientists now believe that *Mesonyx* was in fact a member of the condylarths, like *Andrewsarchus* on page 15. In another 20 years maybe things will have changed yet again...

Mesonyx

Truly a carnivore

Pseudocynodictis was one of the early fissipeds – the true carnivores that are the ancestors of today's cats, dogs, otters, weasels and many other meat-eaters. This slim, swift creature lived around 35 million years ago. It was the size of a large fox and probably led a fox-like way of life, hunting rabbits, rats, mice and other small creatures.

Pseudocynodictis

A TIME OF CHANGE

The Oligocene period, from 38 to 26 million years ago was a time of many changes. After the initial 'burst' of evolution early in the Age of Mammals, the groups were sorting themselves out. There were several surprisingly modern-looking types among the animals. The cats for example – those most specialized of meat-eaters – had developed rapidly, and were already very similar to the cats of today. They and other advancing groups were replacing the 'old-fashioned' mammals such as the creodonts.

Confusingly, some mammals looked like those alive now, but were not close relatives. *Archaeotherium* was like a large pig but it belonged to the entelodonts, a separate group from the one which gave rise to present-day pigs, giraffes, antelopes and other mammals with an even number of toes on each foot.

Other Oligocene animals were the ancestors of species around today, but they had not yet evolved into the typical shapes we would recognise. *Poebrotherium*, no bigger than a sheep, was a small, early type of camel that already had just two toes on each foot – like today's camels.

Some Oligocene creatures – like *Merycoidodon*, which looked like a cross between a pig and a sheep – were very successful at the time, but died out. The Oligocene was an interesting phase in mammal evolution, and it presents palaeontologists with plenty of puzzles.

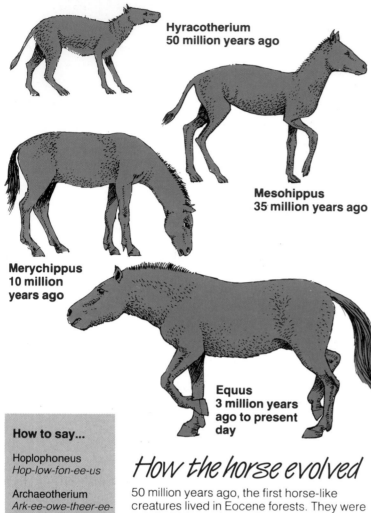

**Hyracotherium
50 million years ago**

**Mesohippus
35 million years ago**

**Merychippus
10 million
years ago**

**Equus
3 million years
ago to present
day**

Horses, rhinos and tapirs

The great Oligocene success story involved the group of mammals which are called 'perissodactyl ungulates' – hoofed mammals with an odd number of toes on each foot. These are the horses, rhinos and tapirs. During the Oligocene they flourished in a way that has never been seen before or since.

When we gather together all the fossils of a certain group, such as horses or rhinos, it is tempting to arrange them in an 'evolutionary tree'. We may expect the tree to be nice and neat, with just a few tidy branches. We imagine one species evolving into another, which is the ancestor of the next, and so on, in a line up to the present day.

Unfortunately, nature is rarely so straightforward. The simple 'tree' is in reality a complicated, twiggy bush. The fossils we find are only the tips of a few twigs; the rest is guesswork based on the evidence discovered. And even though we can place animals in an 'evolutionary line', like the rhinos shown opposite, this does not mean that each creature in the line is the ancestor of the one after it. Sometimes they may be. In other cases they probably aren't. We can never know for sure. If someone digs up a completely new kind of fossil the experts may have to draw up the evolutionary trees all over again.

How to say...

Hoplophoneus
Hop-low-fon-ee-us

Archaeotherium
Ark-ee-owe-theer-ee-um

Poebrotherium
Poe-ee-bro-theer-ee-um

Merycoidodon
Merry-coy-doe-don

Hyaenodon
High-een-owe-don

How the horse evolved

50 million years ago, the first horse-like creatures lived in Eocene forests. They were only just bigger than a domestic cat, with five tiny nails on each foot.

Fossils through the ages show that members of the horse group gradually became bigger, with longer and thinner legs. The number of toes on each foot was five, then three, and today it's one – the horse's hoof. The teeth and jaws became bigger and better at dealing with tough foods such as grass. Today the wild horse is a fast-moving, plains-dwelling, herd-living creature.

Nightfall at an American river during the Oligocene

1 Hoplophoneus *was an early sabre-toothed cat. Its long canine teeth were used to stab and kill its prey.*

2 Archaeotherium *had tusk-like canine teeth. Fossilized examples suggest that it may have used them to dig and grub up roots.*

3 Poebrotherium *was a very early kind of camel. It was only 50 cms tall at the shoulder.*

4 Merycoidodon *has no descendants living today. Its teeth show it to be related to cud-chewers like cows.*

5 Hyaenodon *was a meat-eating creodont. It was large and heavily built, like today's wolves.*

6 *Prehistoric bats flitted over the dark river, searching for flies and other insects. Bats had already been around for millions of years.*

Rhinos through the ages

Rhinos developed from an early tapir-like animal and the prehistoric ones came in all shapes and sizes. Some didn't have horns, others had one or more. Of the dozens which have lived in the past, there are only five species left alive today. They are all rare, partly because they are hunted by humans. It would be terrible if we were responsible for making them extinct, so finishing the 'rhino tree' for ever.

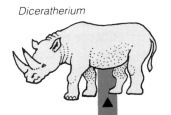

Diceratherium

African white

Today's rhinos
There are only five species of rhino alive today. These are the *Sumatran, Indian, Javan* and the *African black* and *white* rhinos.

Tapir ancestor

Caenopus

Mainstream rhinos
The main 'branch' of rhino evolution started with animals like *Caenopus*, which was about 2.4 metres long. It had three toes on each foot, large front teeth, but no horn. For millions of years rhinos were like this – heavy bodied, browsing, thick-skinned creatures. One, *Diceratherium*, had two horns.

Indian

African black

Tapir

Giant hornless rhinos
One side-line from the main branch of rhino evolution were giant hornless rhinos – like *Paraceratherium*.

Javan

Sumatran

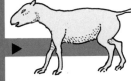

Running rhinos
One rhino group became more horse-like and able to run swiftly. The running rhino *Hyracodon* was about 75 cms tall, lightly built, with long legs and three hoofed toes on each foot. Like many primitive rhinos, it had no horn.

Woolly rhinos
During the Ice Age, some rhinos developed long, thick coats to keep out the cold. They became extinct only a few thousand years ago.

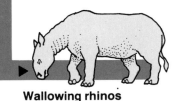

Wallowing rhinos
The wallowing rhinos were an offshoot from the running rhinos. *Metamynodon* was rather typical of this group – rather tubby and short-legged. We think that they swam and wallowed in water, much like hippos do today.

Grazing rhinos
A few of the later rhinos specialized in grazing. They included *Elasmotherium,* which had very strong grinding teeth. This was the largest of the horned rhinos, with a huge horn 2 metres long on a strong skull 1 metre long.

LIFE ON THE PLAINS

The animals that live in our modern world are greatly affected by the plants growing in their environment. This was also true during prehistoric times. During the long period called the Miocene, which was from 26 to 7 million years ago, grasses became important plants. This was because the climate in many parts of the world became drier, so the drought-resistant grasslands spread as the rain-loving forests died back.

As the plants changed, so did the animals. Shady forest glades with their succulent leaves, shoots and fruits gave way to open plains of tough grass, which needed equally tough teeth to make use of it. It was a case of 'browsers out, grazers in'. Many of the old-style browsing mammals became less common and new types, grazing on the grasses and other ground-growing plants, took over.

At the start of the Miocene there were still many types of rhino, but the other main group of odd-toed hoofed mammals, the horses, became much more widespread. The even-toed hoofed mammals also became numerous, many of them living in herds.

By the end of the period plains-dwelling herbivores such as antelopes were in existence, along with deer and giraffes. A new selection of carnivores evolved to prey on these new plant-eaters. The world was changing, and the mammals, ever adaptable, were changing with it.

The dawn of Darwin's Ideas

Darwin's voyage
Darwin travelled to South America and the Pacific on a ship called the Beagle. *The map on the right shows its passage around South America and the Galapagos Islands.*

On the shores of Patagonia, Darwin found many fossils, as you can see in the picture below. He dug up the fossilized bones of lots of extinct animals and study of these led him to form his theories about evolution.

Nowadays nearly all palaeontologists accept the general idea of evolution. We almost take it for granted that animals and plants gradually change with time, as one generation follows another. Sometimes a particular kind of animal becomes extinct or changes into a completely new and different species.

One of the main reasons we believe in the idea of evolution is that we can imagine how it happens. As the world slowly changes, it suits some animals better than others. These well-adapted types thrive, while others die out. We call this 'the survival of the fittest', and we owe the idea to the naturalist Charles Darwin.

In 1831 Darwin sailed round the world on a ship called the *Beagle*, which spent five years mapping the coasts of South America. The things that Darwin saw convinced him of the theory of evolution, even though people laughed at his ideas. He visited the Galapagos Islands, where he saw a variety of closely-related living species, and spent time in South America where he found many wonderful and unique mammal fossils. These were the most important parts of his voyage.

Darwin saw at first hand just what odd and gigantic animals had lived in the area called Patagonia, and this set him thinking about how and why animals became extinct. He also studied the